This book belo

_____

On Christmas Eve, Santa gathered his reindeer together to leave for the big night.

They had many children to visit and Santa looked forward to the evening with his hard working reindeer.

Next was Cathleen Brooke. She was having a hard time at school because she had just moved there.

Before you knew it, he had landed in Antarctica where no children lived.

Santa felt crushed. He knew so many kids were depending on him. But without any light, he wasn't going to be able to finish his routes.

Fritz didn't know what he had done. He just remembered having too many of Ms.Claus's burritos.

23828202R00021